GARFIELD

TREASURY 2

JIM DAVIS

Based on "The Sixth Garfield Treasury"
and "The Seventh Garfield Treasury"
(© 1991, 1993 Paws, Incorporated)

This edition first published by Ravette Publishing Limited 2001.

Printed and bound for Ravette Publishing Limited,
Unit 3, Tristar Centre,
Star Road, Partridge Green,
West Sussex RH13 8RA
by Gutenberg Press Ltd, Malta.

ISBN: 1 84161 042 9

OH, VERY WELL, GARFIELD, YOU MAY HAVE MY STEAK

I KNOW. I'M A SUCKER FOR THE LOVING ADORATION OF A PET

JPM DAVPS

1-22

© 1989 PAWS, INC. All Rights Reserved. 1-29

JIM DAVIS

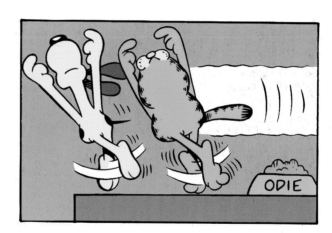

4-2 JIM DAVIS

I DON'T KNOW WHAT GOT INTO MY CAT! I'M REALLY SORRY!

NONSENSE! THAT'S THE MOST EXERCISE REBA'S HAD IN 4EARS!

WHY CATS ARE LAZY...

CAT'S POINT OF VIEW

© 1989 PAWS, INC. All Rights Reserved.

WHY CATS NEED HELP...

CAT'S POINT OF VIEW

WHY CATS HATE DOGS...

CAT'S POINT OF VIEW

JIM DAVIS 5-14

AND WHY CATS ARE VAIN...

A CAT'S FAVORITE VIEW

JIM DAVIS

7-2

WHAP!

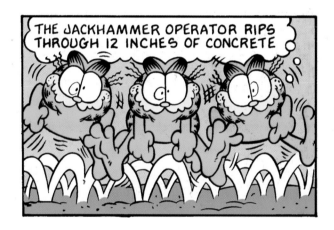

JIM DAVIS   8-13

JIM DAVIS

9-3

10-1   JIM DAVIS

JIM DAVIS   11-5

THIS CHAIR ISN'T LEVEL

THUNK THUNK

THAT'S EASY ENOUGH TO FIX

KACHINK- KACHINK-

© 1989 PAWS, INC. All Rights Reserved.

KACHINK- KACHINK- KACHINK-

KACHINK- KACHINK- KACHINK-

KACHINK- KACHINK- KACHINK-

JIM DAVIS   11-19

GARFIELD!!!

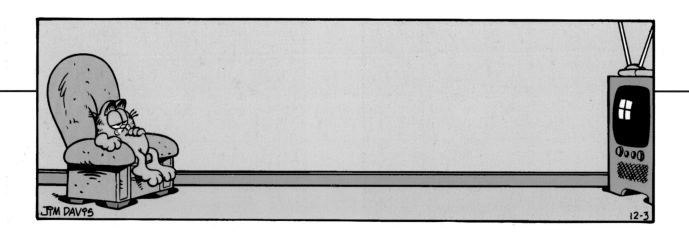

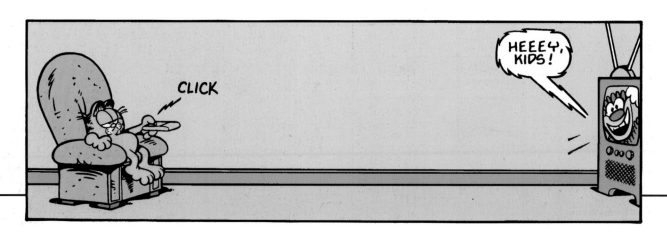

PAT
PAT
PAT

PAT
PAT
PAT

JIM DAVIS

1-7

JRM DAVIS

SHOOF

SHOOF

SHOOF

1-14

ALL RIGHT! ALL RIGHT!!
I'LL FIX YOUR BREAKFAST!!!

JM DAVIS   2-25

JIM DAVIS 10-14

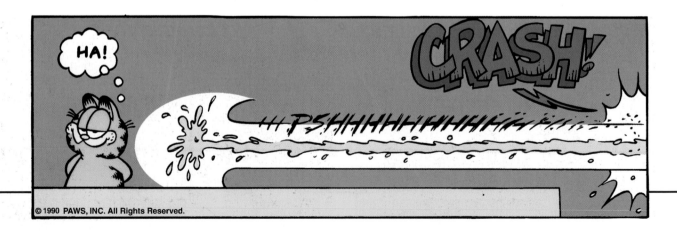

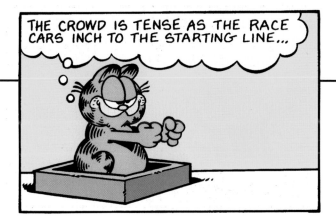

THE CROWD IS TENSE AS THE RACE CARS INCH TO THE STARTING LINE...

SCOOT SCOOT SCOOT

© 1991 PAWS, INC. All Rights Reserved.

AND AS THE STARTING LIGHT FLASHES GREEN, OUR HERO PUNCHES THE GAS!

SHOOM!

JIM DAVIS 3-3

GRRRRRR

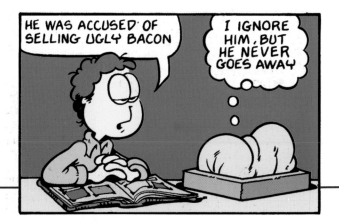

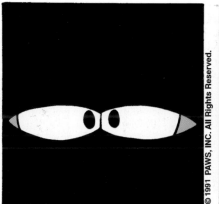

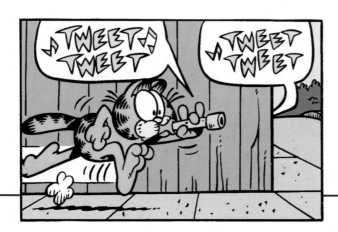

© 1991 PAWS, INC. All Rights Reserved.

JIM DAVIS

5-26

JIM DAVIS 8-4

ARE YOU BOYS QUITE DONE?

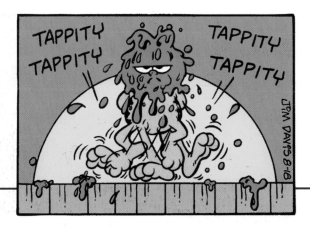

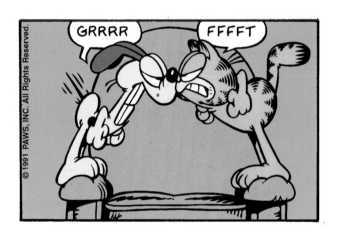

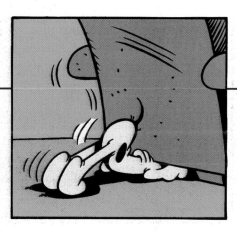

JIM DAVIS 1-19

HELP! CHAIR! HELP! CHAIR!

NEVER SEEN A CHAIR GO BAD LIKE THAT BEFORE

BACK IN '39 I HAD A HASSOCK WITH AN ATTITUDE

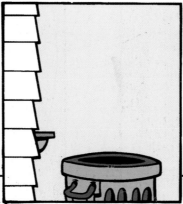

THROW THE BALL, GARFIELD

JIM DAVIS 5-10

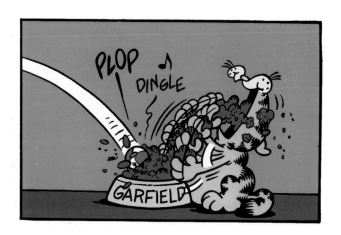

GOOD MORNING, JON!

JIM DAVIS 8-23

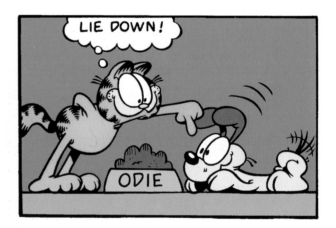

JIM DAVIS 12-20

© 1993 PAWS, INC. All Rights Reserved.

HURRY! HURRY UP AND PERK!!!

PLUP PLOOP